BAKELITE JEWELRY
The Art of the Carver

LYN TORTORIELLO AND DEBORAH LYONS.
PHOTOGRAPHY BY LYN TORTORIELLO

4880 Lower Valley Road Atlgen, PA 19310

Copyright © 2008 by Lyn Tortoriello & Deborah Lyons
Library of Congress Control Number: 2008920389

Designed by John P. Cheek
Cover design by Bruce Waters
Type set in Engraver's Gothic BT/Zurich BT

ISBN: 978-0-7643-2914-2
Printed in China

Schiffer Books are available at special discounts for bulk purchases for sales promotions or premiums. Special editions, including personalized covers, corporate imprints, and excerpts can be created in large quantities for special needs. For more information contact the publisher:

Published by Schiffer Publishing Ltd.
4880 Lower Valley Road
Atglen, PA 19310
Phone: (610) 593-1777; Fax: (610) 593-2002
E-mail: Info@schifferbooks.com

For the largest selection of fine reference books on this and related subjects, please visit our web site at
www.schifferbooks.com
We are always looking for people to write books on new and related subjects. If you have an idea for a book please contact us at the above address.

This book may be purchased from the publisher.
Include $3.95 for shipping.
Please try your bookstore first.
You may write for a free catalog.

In Europe, Schiffer books are distributed by
Bushwood Books
6 Marksbury Ave.
Kew Gardens
Surrey TW9 4JF England
Phone: 44 (0) 20 8392-8585; Fax: 44 (0) 20 8392-9876
E-mail: info@bushwoodbooks.co.uk
Website: www.bushwoodbooks.co.uk
Free postage in the U.K., Europe; air mail at cost.

CONTENTS

ACKNOWLEDGMENTS _____ 4

THE ART OF CARVED BAKELITE _____ 5

   CARVING—VINTAGE VERSUS NEW _____ 6

   COLORS _____ 6

   VALUES _____ 6

INSIDE THE JEWEL BOX _____ 8

RESOURCES _____ 188

SUGGESTIONS FOR FURTHER READING _____ 189

ACKNOWLEDGEMENTS

We wish to thank the following Bakelite enthusiasts, who very generously lent us pieces to be photographed: Lori Kizer, Abby Nash, Sheila Parish, Colleen Shelton, Michael Weinstein, and Joan Young. For contact information, see the "Resources" section at the end of the book. Doug Congdon-Martin and Bruce Waters, of Schiffer Publishing, were unfailingly generous with their expertise. Nancy and Peter Schiffer remain the best publishers an author could wish for.

THE ART OF CARVED BAKELITE

The intricate and spirited carving seen in many vintage Bakelite pieces has long been a source of fascination to us. While admiring the boldness of geometric pieces and the whimsy of figural pins, we also find ourselves drawn to those pieces that illustrate the extraordinary skill of the finest Bakelite carvers. This is demonstrated by the deeply carved pieces with extravagant flowers and leaves, the dense textures, and the swoops and curves that are so characteristic of high-quality pieces of the 1930s and 1940s. The seemingly countless patterns are a testament to the originality of the designers and the skill of the carvers. While we do not know the names of these artists, we honor them here by showing the products of their artistry.

The extraordinary richness of the Bakelite design vocabulary is staggering. Any thoughts we once had of assembling a complete compendium of Bakelite patterns were dashed on a weekly basis, when we saw yet another pattern for the first time. Instead we present a somewhat personal array of our favorites, including many familiar ones and some rarely seen. Because our focus here is vintage Bakelite patterns, we show as many related pieces as possible. Seeing the same pattern compressed or extended to fit shapes as disparate as a bangle and a pendant gives a new perspective on the carver's vision and craft. We have also tried to show patterns in as many colors as possible. On the other hand, some pieces are so unusual that we show them even if they must stand alone.

We avoid using the terms "parure" and "demi-parure," because it is hard to know exactly what pieces were available in any particular pattern. A complete line might have included bangles in as many as three or four widths, a hinge bracelet (sometimes in more than one version), small and large dress clips, one or two brooch shapes, earrings, a pendant, a ring, a two-piece buckle, and sometimes buttons. Other kinds of bracelets, like stretchies and link bracelets, seem to have had fewer matching pieces, but pins and clips can be found. We've gotten close, but haven't yet assembled a complete set of any one pattern. In a few cases like the "leaf on leaf" pattern (see pages 42 and 43) we have found nearly every piece, but in different colors. For the obsessive collector (and here we speak from experience!), this can be a rewarding approach to building a collection.

Bracelets and pins continue to be the most sought-after (and expensive) items, but we have chosen to show a wide range of other pieces. Two-piece buckles, with their large surface area, offer a particularly attractive canvas for carving. Small button earrings show the design elements reduced to essentials. Pendants and rings are relatively rare and desirable. Dress clips, designed to be worn on necklines, were once very popular but have suffered from changes in clothing styles. We are very fond them, since they represent a great inventory of design and can be worn in many ways – on a pocket, clipped to a safety pin as a brooch, on a chain as a pendant. They are still quite reasonable in price, and may therefore be a good choice for the beginning collector.

Carving – Vintage versus New

Every item in this book is at least 50 years old, and most date to the 1930s or 1940s. Today the art of Bakelite carving has been revived by artists, such as Ron and Esther Shultz and Brad Elfrink, who use original Bakelite material with their own elegant designs. These items are collectible in their own right. Signed and sometimes dated, they do not pretend to be vintage. On a less happy note, fake bangles and pins have come pouring onto the market in the last decade. If you want to learn how to test for authenticity, see our earlier book, or Karima Parry's *Bakelite Bangles*. The best defense against fakes, however, is intimate knowledge of the look of fine vintage Bakelite, and familiarity with the patterns and colors. Spend your time, as you are doing now, before you spend your money. Study vintage Bakelite in books such as this and the wonderful books we've listed in Further Reading. Armed with the knowledge of what is "right," you will be prepared when you see something that seems "wrong."

Colors

We use many of the color terms codified in Parry's *Bakelite Bangles*, which have deservedly become the standard when referring to Bakelite colors. Since we have noticed that a few terms – namely "apple juice," "root beer," "creamed corn," and "butterscotch" – are often used improperly, we decided to put the matter to rest once and for all. (See pages 139, 150, 186, 187)

Values

We give a range for most items, indicating low to high retail values. A sharp-eyed collector may be able to pick up some of these pieces for much less, but if you buy guaranteed vintage Bakelite from an established dealer at a show or high-end shop, these prices are what you can expect to pay. A wide range will be found especially with the smaller pieces, like earrings or clips, which may be highly valued by some collectors but which do not have the mass appeal of bangles or pins. A pair of matching clips (especially if mirror images of each other) is worth more than twice the value of a single clip. Similarly, a set of matching pieces (e.g. a bangle and brooch) is worth more than the total of each piece alone. If you find several matching pieces that have clearly been together since their creation, it is much better to keep them together, as this enhances their value. They will usually have been stored under the same conditions and their color will have oxidized at the same rate. On the other hand, a "married" set – if the color and carving are closely matched – is nearly as good

Values are for clean and undamaged pieces. They may show a bit of surface wear such as an even layer of fine scratches that testifies to their age, but chips, cracks, gouges, deep scratches, and the like seriously compromise value. Transparent Bakelite and Prystal pieces often show internal crazing. If it is not severe and does not threaten structural or design integrity, it may be tolerable, especially if the piece is rare or very well executed, but a piece with crazing is still worth less than one without it. Be sure to store your transparent pieces away from extremes of heat and cold to protect them from this kind of damage.

An avid Bakelite collector, Austin J. Austin, has shared this observation: "These ornate carvings would be gorgeous no matter what the medium. Bakelite was ridiculously cheap but the carving has made it timeless. I have observed that the value of Bakelite remains high for the sake of the craftsmanship, not because of the raw materials."

In our previous book, *Plastic Bangles*, we wanted to cover everything we knew about plastic jewelry, its history, how to identify it, where to find it, etc. In this book, we take the exactly opposite approach. This book is all about the pieces. Nothing is in these pages that we do not love, or at least admire for the skill with which it was done. The colors, textures, and patterns of these pieces deserve close study, as would any other artwork. We invite you to enjoy them along with us.

INSIDE THE JEWEL BOX

The preceding pages show an array of pieces in one of our favorite patterns, featuring bold flowers with delicate fringes around the edges. These pieces consist of two separate pieces of Bake-lite bolted together, and are found in an incredible range of colors from opaque to translucent to transparent. The pair of red transparent clips still has its original price tag and it's enough to make one weep -- $1.00 for a pair! Nowadays, expect to pay $25-45 for a clip, $50-100 for a buckle, $25-45 for earrings, $100-250 for a pin, and $350-600 for a hinge bracelet.

Smooth, glowing apple juice and dark red flower
and leaf patterned hinge bracelets, $250-450; large
clip, $60-95; small clip, $25-55; earrings, $25-45.

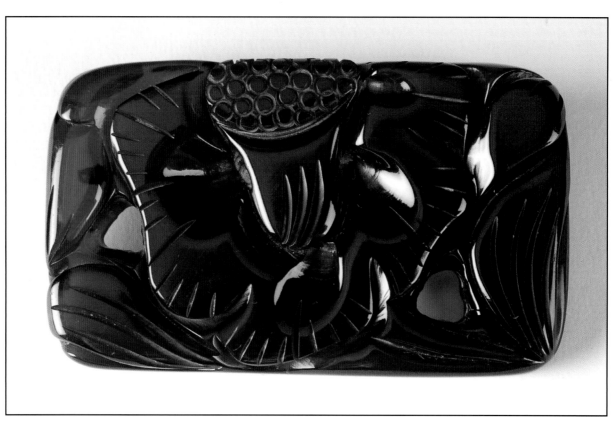

Top: luminous translucent daffodil pattern pin in dark green, $250-400. Bottom: dark blue changer set of pendant, $100-150, and matching clips, $60-95, in a different pattern but with a similar style of carving.

14

A deep red translucent set in the daffodil pattern. Hinge bracelet, $300-450; pair small clips, $60-95; large clip, $70-100; two-piece buckle, $50-100; pin, $250-400.

Top: marbled green bar pin with intricate carving, $125-175. The grape clip has a transparent blue-green wash, $75-125. Root beer transparent and olive translucent clips, $65-95. Bottom: translucent spring green floral carved buckle with Bakelite hasp, $65-85; pair small clips, $45-55; oval pin, $85-125; two-piece buckle, $45-65.

Dark red matching buckle, $85-125; pin, $175-200; vaseline green leaf buckle, $75-95.

A stylized rose pattern with piercing. Hinge bracelet, $300-450; clip, $35-45; pin, $200-350. The pair of red clips, $75-100, is in the same pattern as the pieces above and on the following page. The hinge bracelet, $350-500 has an attached floral piece in a pattern of the same spirit.

Pierced rose pattern: green pendant, $125-175; butterscotch pin, $175-275; green two-piece buckle, $80-100; dark red brooch, courtesy Sheila Parish. Brooch in blue moon, $200-350.

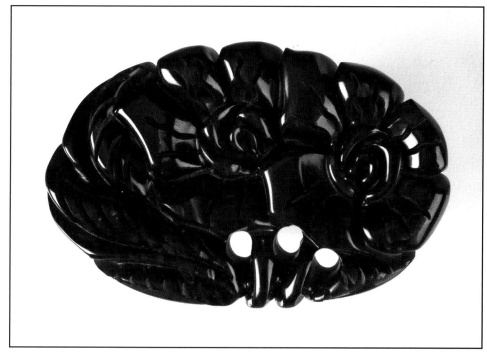

Translucent burgundy set in a flowing stylized floral pattern. Hinge bracelet, $300-450; pin, $200-275; clip, $35-45.

Top: Intricately carved hinge bracelet, $450-650, courtesy Sheila Parish, with similarly carved translucent pin with scrolled leaves, $175-250. Bottom: pierced green translucent circle pin, $200-350.

A very deeply, heavily carved lotus pattern, in translucent green. The facing page shows a wide range of pieces and colors in this same pattern. Note the pronounced differences in carving in the two bracelets. Hinge bracelets, $250-375; earrings, $25-45; two-piece buckle, $75-125; clips, $45-65; pins, $175-250.

These delightful flower pieces are carved even along their edges. Carnelian translucent pin, $95-150; apple juice two-piece buckle, $75-100; pair of creamed corn clips, $65-95. Bottom: chunky cream bangle in leaf and dot pattern, $275-350.

A luminous stack of translucent red and caramel carved bangles, $200-450; Top two, courtesy Sheila Parish.

Cream pierced floral pin, $250-350, courtesy Sheila Parish. Red flowers in a pot, with fluffy cotton centers and some remaining green paint on leaves, $250-350. Approximately 2 ¾ inches high.

Large pierced pins in related swirling floral patterns. Cream pin, $850, courtesy Sheila Parish. Red pin with snake, $350-450. These are each more than three inches across.

Three matching hinge bracelets with an unusual leaf-shaped closure, $575 each. Courtesy Sheila Parish.

Top: stack of heavily carved bangles, $350-600, courtesy Sheila Parish. Bottom: leaf pattern with zigzag edges. Pairs of clips in butterscotch and carnelian (which show pink when held to the light), $65-90, earrings, $25-40, green bar pin, $95-135.

Three lobe-carved bangles, two with worm carving, red with floral carving, $350-550 each, courtesy Sheila Parish.

Left: two bangles, $300-400, and matching buckle, $50-75 in a charming pattern of small over-lapping circles. Above: bold red leaf pin with small circles, four inches in length, $250-325.

Above: fabulous and rare translucent blue moon feather and small dot-carved bangle, $1100, courtesy Sheila Parish. Left: group of pieces in various feather patterns. Green two-piece buckle, $70-95; round dark red pin, $125-175; clips, $35-55.

Stack of leaf and dot carved bangles, $300-550. Bottom bangle, courtesy Sheila Parish.

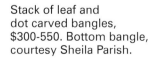

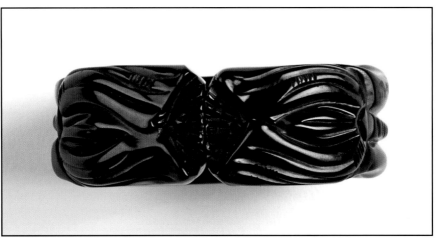

These two pages show one of our favorite patterns – a stylized flower in a fluid art nouveau motif. Pin, $125-225; small clip, $35-45; hinge bracelet, $200-275; two-piece buckle, $65-95; large clip, $65-85.

Matching flower pin and pendant with reverse-carved apple juice, layered with translucent Bakelite and rhinestones. Pin, $350, courtesy Lori Kizer; pendant with original celluloid chain, $250-325. Ribbon carved apple juice bangle with apple juice cabochons, $300-350.

Orchid-like pattern in an array of transparent colors. Hinge bracelet, $375-500; large clip, $65-85; small clip, $35-45; earrings, $25-45; pin, $85-145; two-piece buckle, $50-75.

Teal Prystal bangle and clips with purple flashes. Bangle, $300-450; pair of clips, $75-125.

Set of transparent orchid-carved pieces in bright red. Hinge bracelet, $375-500; earrings, $25-45; pair of clips, $75-100; two-piece buckle, $50-85.

Two Prystal pieces carved in a rare and pleasing bird and leaf pattern. Teal two-piece buckle, $100-175; red pin $150-200.

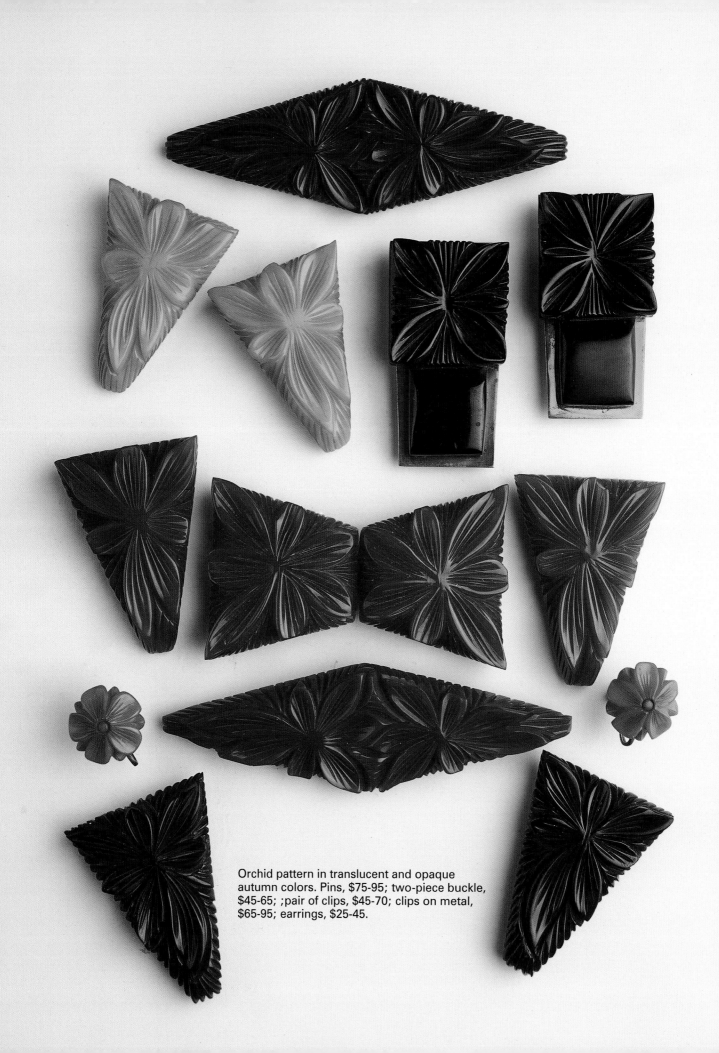

Orchid pattern in translucent and opaque
autumn colors. Pins, $75-95; two-piece buckle,
$45-65; ;pair of clips, $45-70; clips on metal,
$65-95; earrings, $25-45.

A group of carved and laminated clips, including a pair (top) with wood. Single clips, $35-65.

Shown on these two pages is a wide range of pieces in a leaf-on-leaf pattern. Above: black hinge bracelet, $275-350; oval pins, $175-225 each; small clips, $45-65 each. Right: earrings, $35-50, two-piece buckle, $75-100, large green clip, $75-95, red pin, $100-175.

Top: strawberry clips, $75-95
and matching earrings, $40-55.
Bottom: three heavily carved
wide bangles, $175-325.

Top: clover and rose-carved pieces.
Bangles, $125-150; clip, $25-35; ring,
$50-85.
Bottom: acorn-patterned pieces.
Green and carnelian wreath pins,
$150-175 each; buckle, $65-95; green
clip, $75-95; carnelian clip, $55-65;
earrings, $45-60.

Stack of heavily and deeply carved wide bangles in shades of root beer, $275-450.

Group of green and root beer clips. Small single, $20-25; pairs $45-95; large layered clip, $75-125.

A reverse-carved pin and clip, with gold paint and pink glass cabochons. Pin $175-250; clip $75-95.

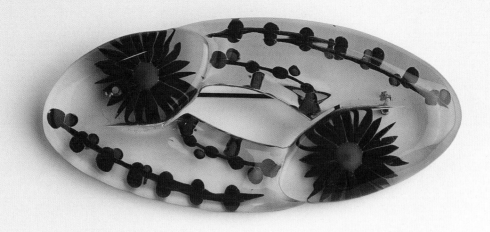

Reverse-carved and painted apple juice pieces. Large oval pin measuring three and three quarter inches in length, $275-350; pin (on left), $65-85; large clip, $75-95; small clip, $50-65.

Three delicate reverse-carved and painted pieces. Bangle, $175-250; pins, $100-175 each.

Top: three carved pieces framed in apple juice. Three-inch long tear-drop with dragon clip, $85-125; orange oval pin, $100-150; green clip, $65-85. Bottom: reverse-carved clip with palm tree, $100-150; large carved clips, $50-75; small clip, $45-55.

Top: unusual wood-framed bangle and large clip with reverse-carved and painted floral design. Bangle $250-350, clip $85-125. Bottom: pair of square clips with dark blue laminated corners and reverse-carved and painted violets, $95-125; reverse-carved and painted pansy laminated with magenta, $65-85; reverse-carved and painted oval clip, $65-85.

Fabulous group of reverse-carved and painted apple juice bangles, $1200-1700, courtesy Sheila Parish.

Apple juice pieces carved front and back with reverse painting. From the top: pin, $85-125; earrings, $35-50; pair of clips, $65-95; rare pair of basket clips with front and back carving, $85-150; front and back carved painted pin, $85-125.

Top: two sets of clips with heavily carved orange centers framed with carved apple juice, $75-125 per pair. Bottom: front and back carved apple juice pieces. Pair of clips, $60-75; leaf clip, $45-60; reverse-carved and painted clip, $50-75; two-piece fan-shaped buckle, $50-75.

Fabulous set of top carved and reverse-painted pieces. Large clip, $75-100;
pair of small clips, $65-95; buckle, $85-100; earrings, $40-60.

Top: huge two and one-half inch top-carved and reverse-painted clip with matching earrings. Clip, $75-100; earrings, $40-65. Bottom: group of red carved clips, $25-55; butterscotch and apple juice reverse-carved pin, $125-175, courtesy Nancy Schiffer.

This group of clips shows a range of techniques including top and reverse carving and lamination. Single-color clips, $35-50; apple juice and red laminated pair, $75-125; apple juice carved framed in black, $45-75.

Above: a group of bangles in a pierced leaf pattern, $150-175, with pierced clips in several patterns, $35-55. Note the unusual blue-green clip in the center. Right: nowhere is painstaking carving more in evidence than on the tiny surface of an earring, usually carved to match a particular bangle pattern, and sometimes a work of art in itself, $35-75.

Top: three pins in a leaf pattern, $75-150. Bottom: group of butter-scotch floral carved pins, $65-95; pair of orange leaf clips in an un-usual pattern, $65-95; green worm-carved clips, $35-60; butterscotch floral clip, $25-40.

Top: two translucent bangles with fine floral and pineapple carving, $125-175; pair of clips $45-75. Bottom: pair of wide matching bangles in a lotus pattern with matching green clips. Bangles, $200-300; pair of clips, $75-125.

Top: an especially large and well-carved pin in a deep translucent emerald green measures 2 7/8 inches high by 1 3/8 wide, and an astonishing ¾ inch thick. $200-275. Bottom: three smoothly carved green bangles in harmonizing patterns, $150-200 each.

Matching pieces in one of the most graceful leaf patterns. Black hinge bracelet, $350-575, courtesy Sheila Parish.
Translucent green and dark red leaf pins, three and one-half inches long, $125-175; pair of clips $50-100.

Top: rare laminated black and green floral pendant with an amazingly sculptural quality. 2 5/8 inches in length. $195-250. Bottom: group of black heavily carved pins. Swan $150-200; layered openwork $130-185; round pierced tree and flowers, $175-225; twig, $85-100.

A stack of heavily and deeply carved bangles, $175-250.
The green bangle on top is tapered towards the back.

These two pages: a group of pieces in a highly stylized and exuberant floral pattern. Apple juice bangle, $200-350; earrings, $40-65; pair of clips, $65-95; buckle, $50-85. The fuchsia set above is stained apple juice. Pin, $175-225; large clip $65-95; pair of clips $85-100.

Right: a stack of green transparent bangles. From the top: green marbled with blue in an unusual daisy pattern with cutaway edges, $275-400; green apple juice with an unusual swirl pattern, $175-300; cloudy green translucent spiral carved, $150-250; spiral carved apple juice stained with green, $150-250. Bottom left: a skillfully carved diamond pattern clip in green Prystal, $65-95. Bottom right: two rhinestone clips of stained apple juice, one with delicate and difficult pierced carving, $50-75.

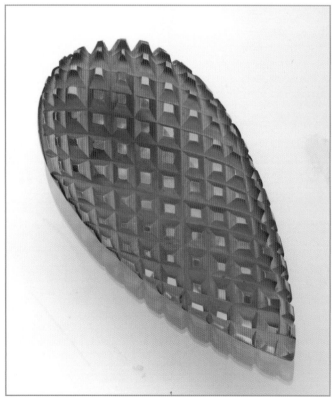

Top: pair of magenta-stained apple juice rhinestone clips, $150-200. Bottom: matching pin and clip in the same pattern, pin $125-195; single black clip $45-65. All rhinestones are channel-set, as is typical of this period.

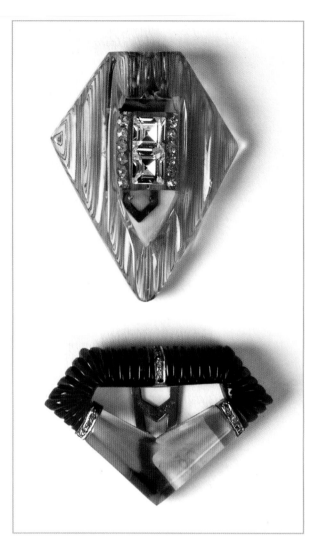

Top: apple juice clip, $45-65; red and apple juice clip, $40-50. Bottom: an impressive and very chunky teal hinge bracelet carved both front and back, with blue rhinestones, $250-400. The color of the bracelet was probably originally closer to the color of the stones, but has darkened over time. Pair of red clips in the same pattern, $85-125.

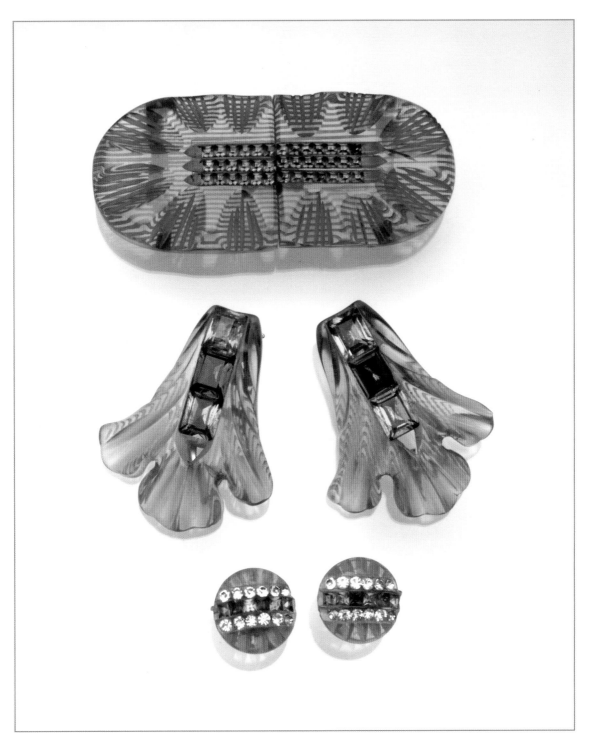

Front and back carved apple juice pieces with rhinestones in a variety of colors. Two-piece buckle with blue stones, $65-85; oak clips, $75-125; very unusual earrings, $45-75.

A group of carved apple juice pieces. Top: bow-tie pin with front and back carving, reverse painting, $150-195. Bottom left: reverse-carved and painted belt buckle, $55-75. Bottom right: pin and matching earrings in a lobe and squiggle pattern. Pin, $95-125, earrings, $40-65.

Stack of carved apple juice bangles. Wide bangles, $300-450; narrow wavy-edged bangles, $50-85 each.

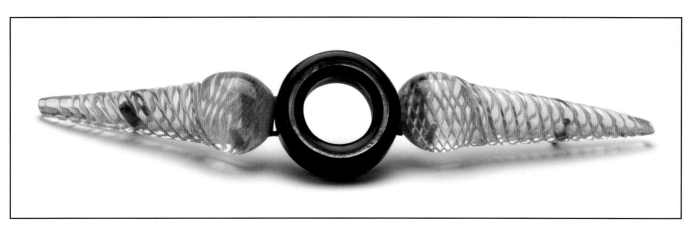

Facing page: a stunning group in black and apple juice, one of the most elegant and flowing patterns, executed in deep rich carving. Hinge bracelet, $350-500; clips, $50-75 each;
pin, $175-225. This page, top: a very rare three-piece buckle with two apple juice pieces
carved in the shape of shells, $125-150. Bottom: hummingbird carved pieces. Teal trans-
lucent hinge bracelet, $350-450; pair of apple juice clips, $85-100; large black clip, $50-65.

Top: a marvelous butterfly buckle with matching buttons. Two-piece buckle, $75-95; buttons $25-45 each. Bottom: reverse-carved and painted fishbowl pin, with fish painted a reddish gold, $375-500.

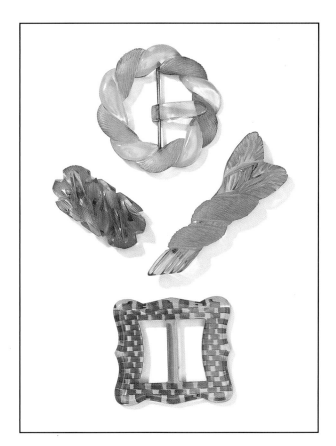

Top: the classic reverse-carved and painted sword-fish and palm pin, $500-850; two palms, $175-200; one palm, $100-150. Bottom: two rib-carved bangles and matching curved clips. Apple juice bangle, $350-450; black bangle, $175-250; clips $45-75.

A group of apple juice carved pieces. Top: round buckle, $40-50; heavily carved textured clip $45-65; unusual arrow-shaped pin, $125-175; rectangular buckle, $35-45. Bottom: apple juice two-piece buckle, $55-75, and matching pin, $65-85, with laminated centers; very unusual pair of apple juice stardust leaf clips stained a brilliant emerald green, $75-100; apple juice carved tear-drop clip, $40-55.

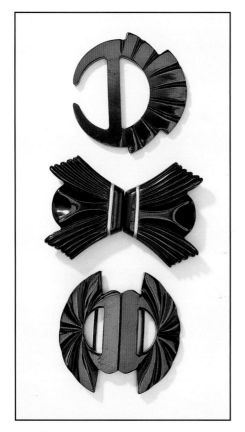

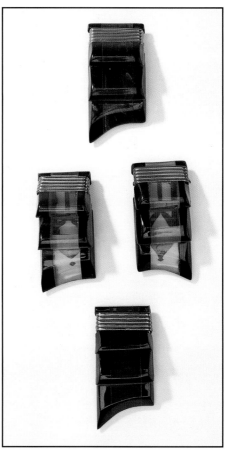

Top left: one and two-piece deco style buckles, $45-75. Bottom left: cape closures, several laminated, $45-75. Top right: a group of finely carved clips, $45-65 each; two-piece buckle, $45-55; feather-carved apple juice earrings, $40-65. Bottom right: laminated ribbon-carved clips in a highly desirable pattern. Pair of apple juice clips, $125-50; single clips $45-60.

Group of buckles, clips, and earrings with different textured patterns. Leaf buckle in black (butterscotch piece is half a buckle), $65-85; six-piece black buckle, $85-125, pair of black clips $45-55; butterscotch buttons $7-12 each; magenta "moderne" design pin $75-95.

Top: a delightful pattern incorporating pierced loops which must have been a real challenge to carve. Pair of clips, $50-85; pin, 150-175; circular clip, $45-65. Bottom: an unusual horseshoe shaped clip, $25-35; two pairs of apple juice Black-Eyed Susan clips, $55-85 a pair.

Top: dark tea-colored bangle, $250-375, and rare teal clips, $75-95, carved in the same pattern, with brass studs. Bottom: a substantial root beer bangle in a lovely undulating pattern, $250-375.

Matching pieces in brick red and marbled dark green, in a
delicate version of the rose and fan pattern. Bangles, $150-175;
wreath pins, $50-75; earrings, $30-55; large clip, $45-65.

Top: a rare, chunky, and beautifully carved example of a rose and fan pattern in vaseline green, $350-475.
Bottom: three matching bangles in a deeply carved floral pattern, $275-375. The transparent teal bangle is harder to find. $350-450.

A group of rose and fan carved pieces, in beautiful translucent and transparent colors. Narrow bangle in marbled apple juice, $125-175; medium width bangle in dark red, $300-400; ring, $95-125; pin, $150-175; two-piece buckle, $125-150.

Pierced rose and fan pattern. Three matching bangles, $150-200 each; black pin, $95-125; red clip, $75-95.

Left: detail of turtle pieces from facing page. Bottom: turtle clips, pins, and earrings in a variety of styles. The tiniest green turtle is a pin, $35-45, and the pair on the bottom are earrings, $35-50; clips $55-85.

Elegantly carved turtles on logs. Hinge bracelets: black with two turtles and blue moon with one, $400-600.
Apple juice clips with black turtles, $100-150 the pair; dark red buckle, $75-100; pin, $150-175; clip, $55-75.

On these two pages: a group of hinge bracelets and matching pieces in a variety of patterns, all adorned with brass wire. Top: pin, $75-95, earrings, $35-55, clip, $35-50. Bottom: black leaf bracelet, $175-225.

Top: green translucent hinge bracelet, extremely well carved, $300-475. Bottom: hinge bracelet, $175-225; clip, $40-55; earrings, $35-55.

Wide black hinge bracelet with double flower pattern, $350-475; dark red pendant in the same pattern, $75-95; round tortoise-shell orchid pattern pendant, $85-100; dark red clip in related pattern, $40-60.

94

Top: cream pin and matching clip are in the same pattern as the hinge bracelet on the facing page. Pin, $200-325, courtesy Lori Kizer. Clip, $50-65. Bottom: orchid-carved pieces framed in brass chain edging. Large green pin, 3 ¼ inches, $200-250, courtesy Lori Kizer; pair of black clips, $65-95.

An unusual pattern featuring stylized glossy low-relief flowers on a matte textured background, framed with squiggle-shaped piercing around the edges. Hinge bracelets, $250-375; green pin, $75-95; pair of clips (translucent magenta), $75-95; black pin, $175-250.

Top: very thick and well carved hinge bracelet in the color of cranberry relish, $375-450, shown with a similarly carved and colored pin, $250-400, courtesy Sheila Parish. Bottom: two lush floral carved hinge bracelets, $300-450.

A group of finely carved green marble pieces. Oval flower pin, $100-150; pairs of clips, $45-55. Center, one of the most unusual and largest clips we have ever seen, at 3 ½ inches high; $100-150. Pin (bottom left), $125-150.

This lovely green set was originally a vibrant aqua color. $175-200 for the set.

Chatting bangles: pair of swirly grooved bangles in pea-soup and butterscotch, $125-150; interlaced brown pattern with piercing, $150-175.

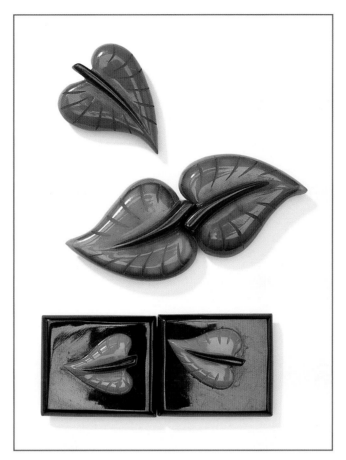

Top: group of laminated leaf pieces. Green clip, $55-65; caramel three-layer buckle, $75-100; green leaves on black, $75-100. Bottom: gigantic moon and stars two-piece buckle, 6 inches across, $85-115.

Top: three elaborately carved and pierced bangles in green and brown. Brown pierced bangle, $500-650, and wide green carved and pierced bangle, $450-600, both courtesy Sheila Parish. Green bangle on right, $375-425. Bottom: stack of chunky green marbled carved bangles, $250-500. Top bangle courtesy Sheila Parish.

Extraordinary carved pierced bangle in lotus pattern (two views), $550-750, courtesy Sheila Parish.

Grape and leaf patterned pieces in deep brown, purple, and two shades of green. Two-piece pin, $75-100; hinge bracelet, $200-300; two-piece buckle, $65-85; bar pin, $75-95; large clip, $55-65; pair of small clips, $50-75. Earrings on following page, $35-50.

Top: see opposite page. Bottom: clips and buckle in a pierced berry and leaf pattern. Large clip, $50-65; two-piece buckle, $65-75; pair of smaller clips, $65-85.

Stack of heavily carved wide bangles, top and bottom in daisy and pineapple pattern, $375-425.

Top: group of daisy and leaf carved clips to match bangles on facing page. Pair of clips, $50-85; large clip, $45-55. Bottom: two curved pins, each four and ½ inches long, in an intricate floral pattern, $150-175.

Group of chocolate carved clips, $45-65, with buckle,
$45-55, and earrings $25-35.

No guilt chocolates: single clips $15-35; stretchy rose-carved bracelet, $125-175.

Top: set of clips and bar pin carved with overlapping circles, pair of clips $35-55, pin $65-85. Bottom: very thick and boldly carved floral pattern. Two-piece buckle, $65-95; pair of clips, $55-75.

This page: aster or dahlia-carved pieces with small circles. Two-piece buckle, $75-85;
pair of blue clips, $55-75; bar pin, $95-125.

Group of leafy pins and clips in red and
black. Black four-leaf pin, $75-95; pair of red
clips, $85-100; remaining pins, $150-200.

Elegant and unusual sucker-carved hinge bracelet and clip set with black laminated edges and brass accents. $725 for the set, courtesy Lori Kizer.

A large and varied grouping of leaf clips. Single clips, $30-45; pairs of clips, 40-75.

This group gives an idea of the wide variety of hardware found on Bakelite clips.

Different patterns with pineapple carving.
Bangle, $200-275; clips, $35-50; earrings, $30-45.

Top: olive and black floral and swirl carved clips and earrings. Clips, $35-60; earrings, $35-45. Bottom: these clips all have interesting deco-style clip backs.

Top: laminated carved pieces: black and cream clip, $45-55; pair of red and cream clips, $60-85; ring, $75-125. Bottom, chunky carved stylized leaf clips, $25-35 each; pair $50-80.

Top: laminated carved clips, $75-125.
Bottom: an interesting group of painted and resin-washed clips and buckle.
Large painted cream clip, $75-95;
black clip, $55-65; resin-washed pair,
$85-120; two-piece buckle, $65-85.

Pineapple and leaf carved bangles with matching clips on facing page. Clips, $45-85; bangles, $165-250.

Facing page: A black bangle and pin in a flower and pineapple design. Bangle, $175-200; pin, $150-175. Above: pineapple and half-daisy pattern. Narrow bangles, $150-185; wide bangle, $275-450; clips, $50-75; oval pins, $150-200.

These two pages: stylized rose pattern in a range of colors. Two-piece buckles, $75-100; pair of clips, $75-95; single clip, $35-45; pendant, $95-125; oval or round pin, $125-150.

Scarf pins have two hinged pieces on top that open to hold a scarf. The blue pin has an additional feature. It is a "Duette" pin; attached to a removable metal pin-back, the two halves slide off to become dress clips. Feather and duette pins, $125-175.

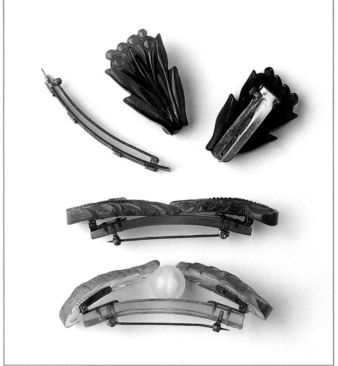

Top: figural scarf pins, leaf, dogs, and birds, $100-175. Bottom: dangle pin with duck, shoe, and butterfly in translucent blue moon, $175-225; squirrel pin, $85-135; bow barrette, $25-45; pair of shoe zipper pulls, $35-45.

Top: shell-shaped clips, $35-55 each; pair of resin-washed clips, $75-95. Bottom: flowerpot pin with green flower, $75-125; green strawberry clip, $50-65; lemon clips, $65-95; laminated tomato earrings, $65-85.

Creatures mythical and otherwise. Top: pair of black scarabs with green marbled wings, clips, $100-125; single black clip, $50-75; green scarab ring, $95-135; beetle earrings, $65-95. Bottom left: green flower on wood and root beer caterpillar on wood, clips, $85-125; butterscotch birds on wood, earrings, $65-85; tortoise deer on butterscotch pin, $200-350. Bottom right: very unusual elephant head clips, $100-150 each, courtesy Abby Nash; green marbled sea monster pin, $175-250; very unusual pink transparent sea monster clip, $75-95.

Top: rare top hat clip, $175-250; hand clips, $85-100 each. Bottom: well carved black hand pin with dangling berries, $275-400; green hitchhiking hand pin with bracelet and painted nails, $500-650; butterscotch hand clip, $85-100.

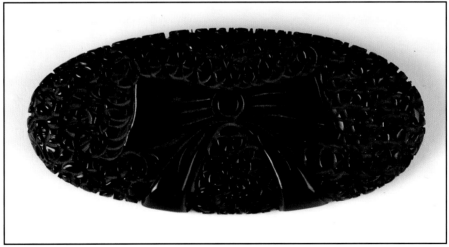

Top: bellflower two-piece buckle, $125-175; pair of blue clips, $100-125; brown single clip, $45-55. Bottom: large black oval pin with bow surrounded by small overlapping circles, 3 5/8 inches across. $250-300, courtesy Lori Kizer.

Group of floral carved pieces in cream, black, and dark green. Bangle with dense carving on the sides, $175-250; round cream clip, $65-85; dark green and black clips, $35-45; butterscotch earrings, $35-45.

Top: three pins in dogwood pattern with piercing, $150-175. Black pin, courtesy Abby Nash. Bottom: large three-layered carved clip, 3 inches wide. $150-195.

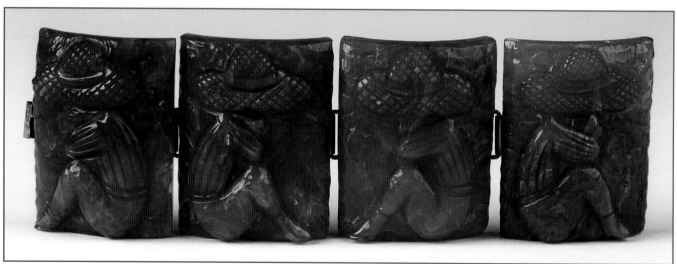

Rare delicately carved link bracelet with figure of resting Mexican, on four plaques, each 2 inches high. $500-750.

Top: Unusual cactus-carved bangle, $450-650. Bottom: chunky bangle, carved with alternating lobes of smooth and bark carving, $350-550. Both courtesy Sheila Parish.

Above: two bangles carved in rose and ribbon pattern, $175-250. Facing page: an ear of corn picks up the color of the accompanying pieces. Originally white and ivory Bakelite has oxidized to the yellow color of corn, known to Bakelite collectors as cream or creamed corn.

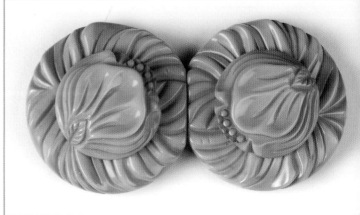

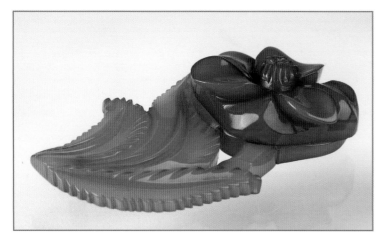

Left: thick and juicy green flower pin, three and ¼ inches in length and up to 5/8 inch thick. The flower is a second layer laminated onto the pin base. $225-300. Right: deep cream buckle with detailed floral carving. The top layered is bolted on. $100-145.

Top: a translucent marbled bangle with deep rose and leaf carving, $300-400, shown with a similarly carved translucent green rose-carved clip, $70-85. Bottom: two bangles in the same pattern, but in different proportions. The narrow blue moon bangle, $150-175; wider green bangle, $250-300.

Right: pair of cleanly styled blue moon leaf clips, $75-100; root beer pin with three leaves, $150-200. Bottom: pair of green maple leaf clips, $70-95; single cream clip, $35-45; buttons, $20-25 each.

Carved green marble flower set, $950. Courtesy Lori Kizer.

Virtuosic carving sets this link bracelet apart. Dark red Bakelite on metal plaques, $275-375.

Left: a group of flower and leaf clips in different patterns surround a philodendron-carved pin and a buckle of brown Bakelite mounted on metal. Clips, $25-50 each; philodendron pin, $125-175; two-piece buckle, $85-95. Bottom: very unusual hinge bracelet with two attached Scotties, $375-500.

A pair of glazed pumpkin bangles, $750 for the pair, courtesy Lori Kizer. Black pinwheel- carved bangle with alternating matte and shiny sections, $275-350.

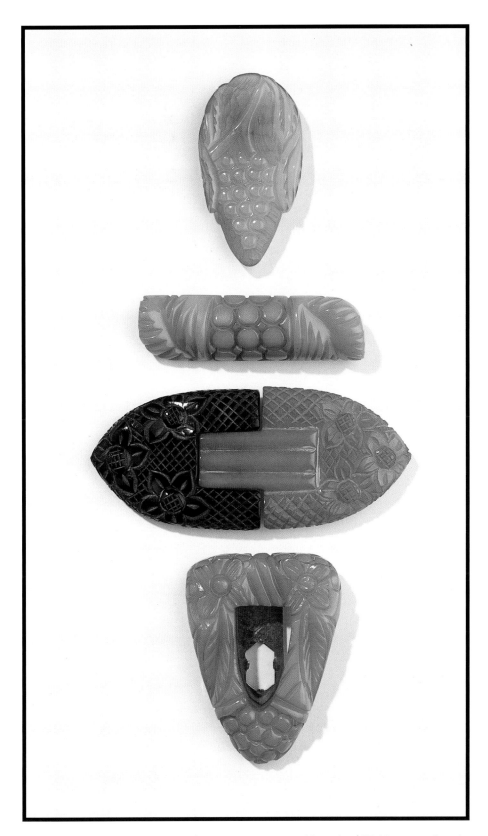

Butterscotch grape-carved clip, $45-55; grape-carved bar pin, $85-95; two-colored delicately carved buckle, $95-135; chunky apricot colored clip, $45-55.

Above: a group of unusual pins and clips. Large root beer pin, three and ¾ inches by two and 3/8 inches, $250-300; two resin-washed root beer clips, $40-50; butterscotch clip, $35-40; butterscotch pin, $175-225. Facing page: butterscotch candies with butterscotch Bakelite. Bangle, $175-250.

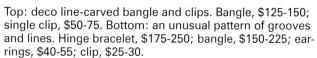

Top: deco line-carved bangle and clips. Bangle, $125-150; single clip, $50-75. Bottom: an unusual pattern of grooves and lines. Hinge bracelet, $175-250; bangle, $150-225; earrings, $40-55; clip, $25-30.

Top: rare worm-carved pattern with raised dots. Set of bangle, large clip, ring, and earrings, $350-400. Bottom: feather and dimple pattern. Bangle, $150-175; orange clip, $45-65; green pin, $125-150.

Top: group of carnelian pieces. Pair of clips with matching earrings, $150-175; bar pin with matching clip, $200-225. Large oval clip with rose carving, $65-85. Bottom: group of olive pieces. Clips on original cards, $45-65 each; earrings, $40-55; two-piece buckle, $75-95.

Top: geometric shapes with heavily carved flowers bolted on. Cream pin, $175-250; single clips, $50-75. Bottom: leaf-carved group. Bangle, $150-185; clips, $25-65; earrings, $35-55.

Deco swirls. Top bangle, $175-250; bottom bangle, $275-350. Clips, $55-75 each; pins, $125-150.

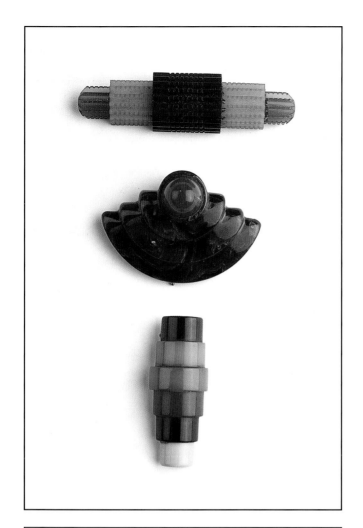

Top: machine age clips. From top, *mardi gras* pin (originally in the *mardi gras* colors of green, gold, and purple, purchased in New Orleans, $150-175; green marbled clip with red dot, $65-85; six-colored clip, $125-150. Bottom: deco clips, $25-35 each.

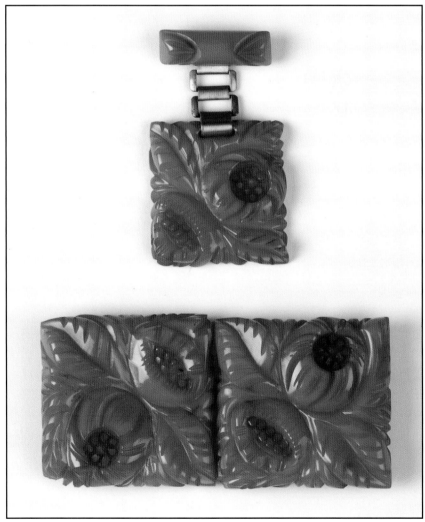

Beautifully detailed frontal lotus design. Top: red hinge bracelet, $375-500; pair of green clips, $75-95; bar pins, $175-225 each. Bottom, shown as a set in pumpkin, two-piece pin and matching buckle, $350-400, courtesy Lori Kizer.

A heavily carved and pierced pattern of flowers and leaves. Two-piece red buckle, $85-100; red hinge bracelet, $350-475; bar pins, $150-175; clips, $45-65 each.

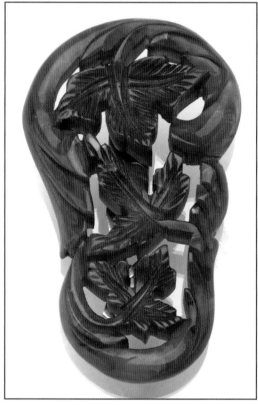

Left: a group of heavily carved pieces in marbled green and dark red. Clips, $45-65; earrings, $35-45; bar pin in center is made up of two layers, with a palm-tree carving on top, $175-250. Right: large carved pierced ivy patterned clip, two and ¾ inches long, $85-125.

Stack of heavily deeply carved sunflower bangles, $325-400 each. Top two, courtesy Lori Kizer.

Top: stylized rose pattern. Transparent green hinge bracelet, $275-350, and matching pendant, $150-175. Dark red clip, $65-75. Bottom: deep wine trans-lucent pieces. Floral clip, $65-75; pair of knot clips, $65-85; earrings, $40-55.

Smoothly carved acorn patterned pieces. Wide bangles in tortoise and transparent deep red, $400-550; double acorn pin, $95-125; clip, $45-65.

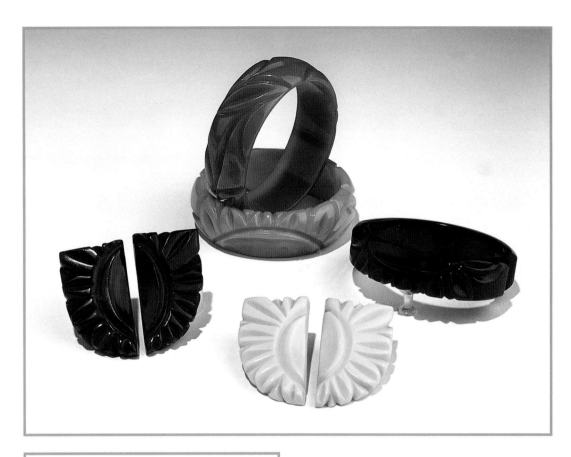

Top: green bangle, $150-175. Stylized sunflower pattern: butterscotch bangle, $150-200; red hinge bracelet with matching clips, $175-225; pair of matching cream clips, $55-70. Left: group of patterns with pineapple carving. Clips, $35-65; bar pin, $95-125; earrings, $25-35.

Top: well carved pieces with fluid lines: chunky red clip, $45-65; butterscotch buckle and matching clip, $75-95; single clips, $35-50; earrings, $35-45. Bottom: three pairs of matching pierced carved clips, $75-95 a pair.

Top: overlapping leaf pattern. Pair of vaseline green clips, $65-85; pumpkin pin, $125-175; large red clip, $55-70; cream clip, $35-55. Bottom: hinge bracelet in apricot, $250-300; matching pin in olive, $145-165; morning glory patterned clip, $55-65; matching earrings in green and orange, $35-45 a pair.

Left: bright brick red earrings, $35-45; two-piece buckle, $65-95. Below: pattern of flower on a stem with leaves. The flowers are layered on with a second piece of Bakelite. Two-piece buckle, $125-150; clip, $65-85; one-piece buckles, $95-125.

Top: boldly carved profile of a woman in a deco style. Oval pin, $175-250; smaller round pin, $125-150; pendant, $175-225, earrings, $45-60. Bottom: Pair of dark red translucent smoothly carved brass-framed clips, $85-100; single clip, $40-50.

Top: dark red carved bird on brass clip, $65-85; heavily pierced floral design pin on brass, $150-175; pair of clips, $55-65; single clip, $45-55. Bottom: gouge-carved petal pattern on textured background. Black triangular clip on brass, $55-65; two-piece buckle with matching clips, $85-100.

Top: translucent dark purple pineapple lozenge pattern bangle, $175-250, clip, $40-60; bar pin, $85-125; earrings, $35-45. These pieces were assembled over time and show different degrees of oxidation. Bottom: pineapple and ribbon-carved bangle with pineapple and groove-carved clip and earrings, all originally lavender oxidized to brown. Bangle, $175-235; clip, $45-55; earrings, $35-45.

Top: deep translucent wine set in a finely ribbed pattern. Bangle, $175-250; pair of clips, $65-85.
Bottom: deco-carved hinge bracelets. Deep translucent wine, $350-500; brown swirl, $300-450.

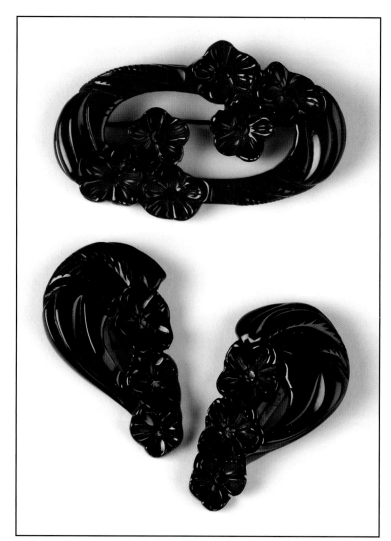

Top: Open floral design with *art nouveau* feeling. Pin, $100-150; pair of clips, $65-85. Bottom: clips in feather and floral patterns with piercing, $35-55.

Top: flower and stem pattern. Buckles, 65-95; blue moon clip, $45-65; apple juice pin, $95-125. Bottom: green marbled and black examples of this extraordinary clip, which measure 2 and 3/4 by 2 ¼ inches, $100-150 each.

Black and apple juice pieces. Two-tone triangular button, $15-20; clips, $45-75 each; two-piece buckles, $45-65; black bar pin, $75-85.

Top: three monogram pins in different styles. Apple
juice pin with pseudo-monogram, $125-150; Butter-
scotch pin with gothic lettering, $85-100; butterscotch
"AK" set into green marbled leaf, $55-65. Bottom: two
berry clips, turquoise with cream leaves and maroon
with green leaves (unsigned Miriam Haskell), $125-175.

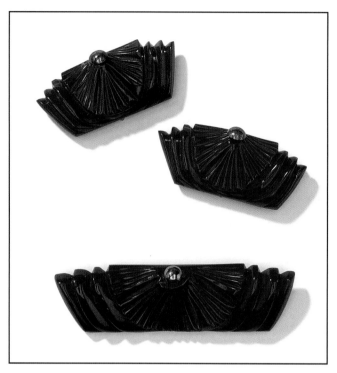

Top: brick red pin and matching shoe clips with brass balls, $150-195. Bottom: three matching resin-washed bangles, $175-200. The purple color is especially hard to find.

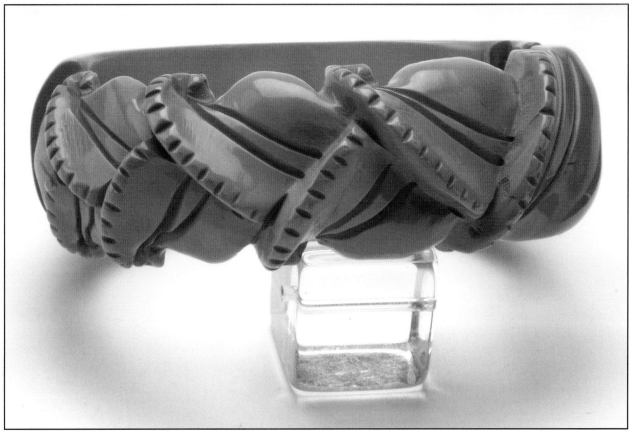

Top: very dark wine translucent heavily carved bangle, $650. Bottom: dark cream hinge bracelet in elegant deco leaf design, $500. Both courtesy Sheila Parish.

Cream heavily pierced and carved bangle, $250-300; carnelian pierced hinge bracelet with dense floral carving, $275-350; brown heavily carved rose hinge bracelet, $450-600, courtesy Sheila Parish.

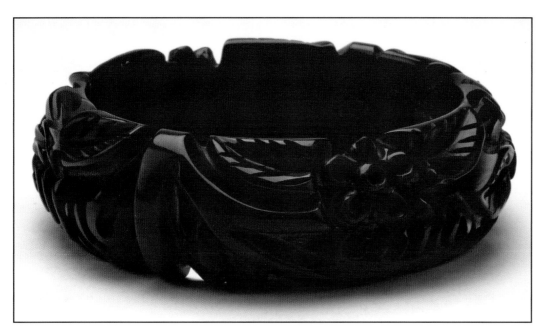

Top and bottom: two views of a fabulously intricate red rose-carved bangle, $800-975. Courtesy Sheila Parish. Center: rare beautifully carved and heavily tumbled translucent golden bangle, $400-550.

Top left: orange two-piece buckle, with framed flower against background of small circles, $75-95, courtesy Michael Weinstein. Bottom left: finely carved orange hinge bracelet in a similar pattern, $450-600, courtesy Sheila Parish. Top right: densely carved tortoise pin, $95-125. Bottom right: Chinese red pin with tropical flowers, $125-150; large butterscotch shield clip with deco leaf carving, $75-95.

Three saucy buckles. Circular with Bakelite hasp, $40-55; two-piece laminated daisy buckle, $100-150; resin-washed leaf buckle with Bakelite hasp, $45-65.

Top left: green bird pin with intact painting. Bottom left: cream pierced floral carved pin, $350-950, both courtesy Sheila Parish. Top right: flock of bird-on-branch clips and pin. Pair of clips, $75-95; single clip, $35-45; pin, $125-175. Bottom right: rare highly detailed frog earrings, $65-95.

Dark green translucent fruit-motif hinge bracelet with matching clips. Hinge $375-575; pair of clips, $60-95.

Three floral pins. Round butterscotch pierced, $125-150; black framed, $125-50; orange daffodil, $175-225.

Top: three well carved two-piece buckles, $65-95. Bottom:
exceptionally well and heavily carved red earrings, $40-60.

Transparent spring green prystal pieces. Front and back carved clip, $45-55; two-piece buckle, $65-85; pair of front and back carved clips, $65-96; large clip with goofus glass center, $65-85.

Group of prystal pieces with carved flowers picked out in white. Set of matching round clip and bar pin in red prystal, $125-175, courtesy Colleen Shelton. Single clips, $40-50; pin, $75-100; ring, $85-125. Pair of lighter green clips with a different pattern, $65-95.

Top: reverse-painted carved green pin with rhinestones, $85-95; red translucent buckle, $65-75; green reverse-painted clip, $55-65; round clips, $45-55 each. Bottom: reverse-carved stained apple juice hinge bracelet, $250-350; two-piece buckle, $45-65, courtesy Abby Nash; clip, $35-45.

Group of rib-carved candy colored pieces.
Clips, $35-55; circle pins, $65-95; earrings,
$35-45; link bracelet, $150-200.

Left: bangle in true apple juice color, $275-350. Bottom: group of transparent clips in apple juice, cognac, and red. Single clips, $25-35; pairs of clips, $50-65.

Golden front and back carved pin,
$75-95; apple juice bar pin, $85-125;
red transparent clip, $45-65.

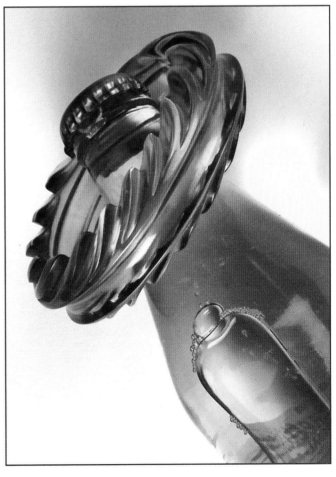

RESOURCES

Lori Kizer, Rhinestone Airplane (www.rhinestoneairplane.com);
    www.lorikizersvintagejewelry.com
Abby Nash, Malabar Enterprises (abbynash@gmail.com)
Sheila Parish, Tutto dal Mondo (tuttodm@aol.com;
    www.antiqnet.com/tutto)
Michael Weinstein, Bundy Museum and Galleries, Binghamton, New York
    (bundymuseum@yahoo.com; www.bundymuseum.com)
Joan Young at Trojan Antiques in Alexandria,Virginia
    (bonnetstobustles@msn.com)

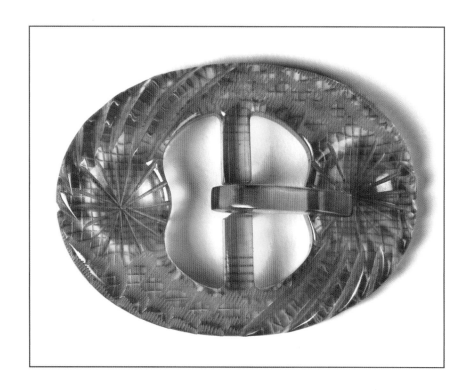

Suggestions for Further Reading

Battle, Dee and Alayne Lesser. *The Best of Bakelite and Other Plastic Jewelry.* Atglen, Pennsylvania: Schiffer Publishing Ltd., 1997.

Burkholtz, Matthew L. *The Bakelite Collection*. Atglen, Pennsylvania: Schiffer Publishing Ltd., 1997.

Davidow, Corrine and Ginnie R. Dawes. *The Bakelite Jewelry Book*. New York: Abbeville, 1988.

Parry, Karima. *Bakelite Bangles: Price and Identification Guide*. Iola, WI: Krause, 1999.

Tortoriello, Lyn and Deborah Lyons. *Plastic Bangles*. Atglen, Pennsylvania: Schiffer Publishing Ltd., 2005.

Wasserstrom, Donna and Leslie Pina. *Bakelite Jewelry: Good, Better, Best*. Atglen, Pennsylvania: Schiffer Publishing Ltd., 1997.